Ice Time

The Game of Hockey and a Journey of Faith

Terry Amann

Foreword by Mike Huckabee

BookLocker

Saint Petersburg, Florida

Print ISBN: 978-1-64719-064-4
Epub ISBN: 978-1-64719-065-1
Mobi ISBN: 978-1-64719-066-8

Published by BookLocker.com, Inc., St. Petersburg, Florida.

Printed on acid-free paper.

BookLocker.com, Inc.
2020

First Edition

Library of Congress Cataloguing in Publication Data
Amann, Terry
Ice Time: The Game of Hockey and a Journey of Faith by Terry Amann
Library of Congress Control Number: 2020920197

All Bible verses in this book were retrieved from:
https://www.biblegateway.com/

Other books by Terry Amann:

Wednesdays with Barry

Dedication and Acknowledgements

This book is dedicated to my wife, Susan Amann, for her love for Jesus and for being my greatest fan.

Many others are to be thanked for their support of this project: Clinton and Samanthya Marlatt; Sarah Amann; Rachel Amann; Levi Wonbenyakeh; Bethany Blankley; Lori Torrano; Pastor John and Barb McWilliams; Pastor Stephen and Florence Wonbenyakeh; Ron and Patti Grams; Kim Hiscox; Larry and Peggy Kenoyer; Ernie and Linda Rudolph; Jeshua and Katie Paris; Parady Boatwright; Donna Dillavou; Chase Robinson; Billy Wilkie; Gary and Syd Arneson; Greg and Kathy Pietraszewski; Jack and Patty Hon; Gary and Shelley Pitts; Randy and Hope Freeman; Rhonda Phillips; Paul and Sally Stout; Darin and Mitzi Wood; Mike Grossman; Sara DeMeulenaere; Jason and Jen Frank; Nadia Frank; Nancy Milton; Gary and Jannell Leffler; Joe and Jeanette Best; Helen Hickman; Emily Andrews; Teague and Brandy Boyd; Clem Duke; Melinda Carriker; Bill and Ramona Clark; Lance and Rasheila Dolleman; Alex and Giselle Petersen; David and Karen Puffett; Sara Hon; Rachel Hon; Jay and Peggy Dillavou; Frank and Crystal Miller; Leah Frette; Tom and Allison Danilovich; Esthervin Mesa Montero; Pat Hall; Arlene Kelly; Church of the Way; The Family Leader; and Mike Huckabee.

Foreword

During times of personal and even national uncertainty, it is often the smallest things that provide the greatest meaning in our lives. It might be the memory of eating peanuts and watching a hockey game with your grandfather, like Terry Amann, or it might be spending time with your family at the beach or camping.

What does hockey have to do with the gospel? Pastor Terry gives us insight into this, and I'm not going to give away any spoilers.

Regardless of whether you've ever played hockey or not, (I certainly didn't growing up in Arkansas), you'll appreciate the life lessons Terry shares from playing the game. We have all experienced times of joy and sadness, or doubt, or just flat out disappointments when we weren't sure what might happen. In hockey, athletes get injured, face major obstacles and challenges. But for many, their love for the game is what keeps them going. They hope to win the ultimate prize with their team but in some cases, they may never reach that goal.

Terry highlights lessons of winning and losing in the game of hockey, and life in general, to ultimately show how we can all win - and in whom we find our ultimate prize. The most important thing we can ever receive isn't obtained through a puck or a stick, but a goal post rooted in grace.

I hope you enjoy this quick read as much as I have and encourage everyone to search for themselves the answers to the questions Terry raises.

Mike Huckabee

Notable Quotes by Hockey Players

"If you play to win as I do, the game never ends."
Stan Mikita

"Orr is the greatest young hockey player that's come along since I've been here."
Bobby Hull

"I'm really no different than anybody else; except that sometimes I get my name in the paper."
Bobby Orr

The author playing a pick-up game of hockey outside
in the frigid cold at the University of South Dakota,
Vermillion, South Dakota circa 1979.

Photo by Susan Amann.

Table of Contents

Introduction 1

Chapter 1 - Intro to Blackhawks Hockey and the Big Question 5

Chapter 2 - Hockey Icons and Tragedies 15

Chapter 3 - Here Come the Hawks 25

Chapter 4 - School and More Hockey 33

Chapter 5 - The Mighty Voyageurs 43

Chapter 6 - Game On! 51

Chapter 7 - Hanging with Hockey Greats 59

Chapter 8 - Madison Street 67

Chapter 9 - Game Off and the Victory of Faith 73

Chapter 10 - Real Champions 83

Pray this prayer from the depth of your soul: 87

Introduction

It's hard to see anything in this dimly lit room. Every time the door opens, a strange waft of sterilized-smelling air blows in from the eerily quiet halls. I can see past my toes, poking out far beyond the end of my bed, into the empty corridors whenever the door opens. A lonely teenager in a children's hospital bed is an experience you never forget.

The television set was turned off several hours ago. I can only hear my breathing and the subtle tick tock of the clock. As I stare at the hands of time making their continual rounds, I count the seconds, waiting for a messenger to arrive.

It seems like hour after hour I'm checking the door until finally, I hear footsteps in the hallway. But it's not him, it's the nurse. She methodically completes her vitals check and leaves. I'm alone again in the room with just my thoughts. In between my glances at the clock and the door, I can't help but think about what I'm doing with my life. After all, I'm a teenager with nothing better to do at that moment other than think about the meaning and purpose of life.

Questions pour into my mind. Why have I had to spend so much time in hospitals? It feels like it's been nothing but surgery after surgery—for years. Is this what it's going to be like for the rest of my life? And what am I doing with my life? Where am I going? And most importantly - what happens when I die? What does any of this mean? Can the Christian Bible provide me with any answers?

Suddenly the hospital door bursts open! The message bearer has arrived! His news won't answer any of my deep questions about the meaning of life or the numerous personal medical trials I will endure. Yet I am desperate to hear about the outcome of something to which I've devoted the last two years of my life: a little black rubber puck.

If I weren't stuck in a hospital bed,

I'd be on the ice playing in a championship hockey game!

The road leading to this championship game was miraculous as you will see. Would I experience other miracles? What could be better I wondered.

This book chronicles my life experiences as they relate to one of the greatest sports games on earth, some lessons I've learned from my family, and how God answered my burning, and not-so-burning life questions. The backdrop for this narrative is the game of ice hockey. For me, hockey has been in the mix throughout my life. Important people who influenced me were also connected to the game. At each new marker in time, I was able to reflect and think about various questions related to life here on earth. Thankfully, I found the answers.

This is my journey. My passion for the Chicago Blackhawks hockey team and my own game experiences will assist me in telling this story. It is my hope this chronicle will assist you to seek and discover the most crucial questions and answers with which we are confronted as mortal human beings. And along the way, you just might come to know and appreciate the game of ice hockey a bit more.

The story begins here...

Chapter 1

Intro to Blackhawks Hockey and the Big Question

At the tender age of four years old, I was sitting on the floor right next to my Grampa Bruni. Grampa had silver hair and wore glasses with black frames. He was medium height and somewhat thin, probably due to his decades long battle with diabetes. Grampa Bruni came from humble Italian and Polish descent. He left home in his teen years and lost track of most of his family. Grampa was a man of few words, a good-hearted soul who collected stamps and wrestled with photography.

Grampa was quietly nestled in the faded-green coarse fabric of *his* over-sized chair. Grampa held a jar of peanuts in his left hand. He would carefully balance the jar on the wide arm of the chair. In his right hand was a fist full of peanuts. That hand dangled over the other side of his royal seat. Grampa seemed to swish the peanuts around in his hand before he methodically brought them to his mouth. He continued to eat peanuts in the same routine, while never taking his eyes off the television screen. I could hear the crunch, crunch, crunch as he ate. When his wrinkled hand was empty, he would scoop more peanuts out of the peanut jar. This would be followed by an occasional wince at the ice hockey action on the screen.

We were watching big screen television. This was not a flat screen, high-definition color digital TV like we take for granted today. Rather, our eyes were glued to a large woodgrain, box-like, black and white Zenith television. Marketing of the day boasted, "The quality goes in before the name goes on," despite the fact that the picture was somewhat grainy. It was, after all, 1963.

Grampa Bruni and I were in the living room at the 4815 West Schubert Avenue Chicago bungalow, home to him and my grandmother, who we called Nana. She was all Italian. Her family settled in upper Michigan where they labored hard as coal miners.

Our grandparents' house was situated on a corner so there was a back alley and a side alley. The garage kept Grampa's yellow 1960 Chevy Bel Air 2-door coupe away from the rigors of the city streets. Chevrolet had taken the famous car fins of the 50's and flattened them on the back end of the car for this model and a new decade.

Across the side alley from their house was a sprawling Dodge car dealership where one night Chicago policemen had a gun battle with armed robbers amidst the new cars in the showroom. We sat up and watched from the porch window with lights blaring and gunfire crackling. The next day we went over to the dealership to count the bullet holes in the large dealership windows.

In addition to being the maternal grandparents of my sister and me, they were also our surrogate parents. Our Mom and Dad married in 1957 but had already gone through the painful throes of divorce. Since we were Catholics then, I can only imagine the shame my grandparents must have experienced as a result of their daughter being divorced. Yet at the time, I had no clue what that all meant.

I was told Dad worked at a job that was far away, which is why we did not live under the same roof. Mom had moved in with her parents, bringing along my sister and me. Mom worked nights as a waitress in an Italian restaurant so she could be home with us during the day. She would head off to her waitress job when our grandparents came home from work. Grampa worked at a jewelry store and also did some moonlighting as a waiter at a fancy restaurant. Nana worked in a factory that built juke boxes.

Growing up in the city of Chicago meant we often sat on the front porch, as did the neighbors. It was a good place to watch the world go by in those days. If you were in the house and friends came to invite you to play outside, they did not come to the door. Instead, they would stand at the base of the backdoor steps and yell, "YO OHHHH Terrrryyyyeee." They never knocked; they just did a yodel until someone came to the door.

We said hello to the postman who delivered mail twice a day by pushing a three-wheel cart with weathered saddlebags stashed with letters. We played all kinds of games on the concrete alley behind our house. One consistent source of trouble was that our ball games in the alley sometimes found the windows of our neighbors' homes. We broke so many windows that finally one day Nana laid down the gauntlet, "If you break another window, you are going to be sent into the army with your Uncle Tim!"

At four years old, sheer terror came over me. And wouldn't you know it, the very next day one of our ball games resulted in a broken window. I was sure I was off to Fort Bragg even though I did not understand exactly what that might entail. In the end, it was a good thing Nana didn't make good on her promise. I was a bit young for the army. Not to mention the fact that my Dad would have insisted on the Marine Corps and absolutely nothing else.

So, my sister and I did not have the full story of how we were born into suburbia and ended up in the Chicago; nor were we silver spoons by any stretch of the imagination. We slept in a room in the attic area which featured an A-frame ceiling. One side of the room had been converted into a nice bedroom. There was a door in the middle which led to the 'creeper' side of the attic. It was dark and foreboding so we never went in there.

There were many times Grampa would hear us giggling upstairs when we should have already been fast asleep. Grampa would stand at the base of the stairs and yell, "Go to sleep *now*! I better not hear another peep! Don't make me come up there!"

Life seemed stable as our grandparents lovingly came alongside our mother and raised my sister and me as their own. They worked hard, did what they could for us, and never complained about the situation. My sister and I still hold fond memories of those very early years.

As a small child and beyond, I had the heavy burden of congenital health issues. I had a deformed eye muscle which was pulling one eye to the side. I had a couple of operations to correct this, but that eye still is not perfect and is very sensitive to light. Glasses of various sizes, shapes, and colors have always been a component of my wardrobe. In addition, we did not know then, but discovered later, that I had dyslexia. In many ways, dyslexia is a silent handicap which other people do not realize you have.

The more challenging health issue was my urinary tract. It was not formed correctly. Surgery was required immediately after birth. This would lead to a multitude of surgeries for the same issue for the next forty-four years of my life. Often those surgeries would leave me feeling like a medical science project.

One of those early surgeries occurred at about the age of three or four. I can still see Grampa Bruni coming to visit me at Children's Memorial Hospital one cold, winter night. I was in a hospital bed with bars so high it seemed like a cage. Grampa had on a long dark trench coat with the collar pulled all the way up, and a fedora pulled down low. He looked like he was auditioning for an old Jimmy Cagney movie. He had the evening edition of the Chicago Tribune newspaper rolled up under his arm. He walked into the children's ward where several other young children and I were convalescing. He didn't recognize me, and I didn't recognize him as he came in and looked around. He did this three times. I finally yelled, "Grampa?" He responded in kind, "Terry?" On that occasion Grampa Bruni looked tired after a long day at work and then having taken public transportation to get to the hospital. Yet, he was very glad to do it.

Clearly, Grampa was an important fatherly figure in my early life. That being the case, it was no surprise to find me by his side, watching the hockey game. I was situated directly across from the living room couch in all its glory. I say that because their large green davenport was made out of the same carpet-like material as Grampa's chair. The big difference was the couch had been enclosed in a heavy, clear plastic cover. That couch was destined to look as pristine on the day it went into the ash heap of history as it was when they first brought it home. If you were wearing shorts in the summertime and you sat down on that couch, your legs would sweat and stick to the plastic.

My aunt and uncle, who lived several blocks away in the same kind of brick bungalow, had the same kind of plastic on their living room couch. No doubt it was a thing at the time, where slick salesmen made sure every brick bungalow in Chicago would have furniture covered in thick, clear plastic.

In front of the couch was a small coffee table. The wood frame was black and the table top was black-and-white marble swirl. The only item on the coffee table was a large, white, ornate Catholic Bible, complete with illustrations. The Bible was always there, although no one ever opened it but me. I would thumb through the pages to look at the pictures of the Bible stories. I did not know it then, but my interest in the Bible was a foretaste of what the distant future held for me.

Few words were spoken between Grampa and me in front of the television. That's because we were watching the Chicago

Blackhawks[1] hockey game. Grampa was very focused on the television when the Hawks were on. The only voice in the room was that of the legendary Blackhawks' announcer, Lloyd Pettit. Everything for him was an exhortation that culminated in, "A slap shot and a goal!"

Lloyd Pettit could bring incredible excitement to the game of hockey like no other. His descriptions of the hockey action, from break-away chances to bench-clearing brawls, would make the hair on your arms and on the back of your neck stand up. A typical hockey fight from Pettit's vantage point would go something like this: "A right hand! Another right hand! An uppercut, and a left! Another right! And down they go!" The description of the altercation on the ice was so vivid that, when overheard on the radio, it was as if you were right there *live*, as an eyewitness with a ringside seat.

The very best of Pettit's vocal cadence was when number 9, Bobby Hull, a.k.a. "The Golden Jet" (with his bold blonde hair), got control of the puck. Chicago Blackhawks fans had a unique love affair with Bobby Hull, one which has endured the test of time and still exists today. Whenever Bobby Hull touched the puck anywhere on the ice, the Chicago Stadium fans would buzz and roar. I have never since seen anything like that kind of emotion with any sports figure. With excitement building on each word, Pettit would chant, "Bobby Hull over the center line... Hull over the blue line... a slap shot and a goal! Bobby Hull, the Golden Jet, has done it again!"

---

[1] At that time, the name 'Black Hawks' was two words. Several years later, the name was changed to Blackhawks, as one word. The latter is used throughout this book for consistency.

Back then, only the away games were televised. Home games were broadcast over the radio with Pettit alone in the radio booth, calling the action. In addition, only the second and third periods were covered live on the radio even though he called all the action from the first period. If a goal was scored or a fight ensued, the audio could be replayed as a highlight of the game.

This was a totally different era of ice hockey, completely opposite the big-money sport it is today. Hockey players would be on the same team for several years at a stretch as free-agency did not exist. In addition to their longevity, hockey players didn't wear helmets so you could see their faces up-close. There were no names on the backs of jerseys, no advertisements on the boards or in the surface of the ice. These were simpler and more frugal times.

I do not remember who the Blackhawks were playing that particular night Grampa and I were watching the hockey game. And I don't even remember if they won the game. What echoes for me, through the corridors of time, is that there was a fatherly figure in our home. Grampa was a hard-working man who always tried to follow the right and honest way. His love, his presence, and his interests would shape my character and my interests, throughout my life. One of those interests would become a passion. That passion was hockey – Chicago Blackhawks hockey.

Still there was one area of Grandpa's life I did not understand. It had to do with church. On Sunday mornings Grampa would drive Nana, Mom, my sister and me, to St. Genevieve Catholic Church which was just a few blocks from home. Grampa would pull up in front of the church and drop us off. After church, he would be there to pick us up, but he never went inside. His absence in the pews was never discussed so that was just how it was.

I did not understand why we went to church, but even from my young vantage point I could tell that it must be important. Plus, I knew there was a God because people talked about Him and the big coffee-table book somehow told His story. Years later, I would learn what Jesus said in the Bible about the strength of the church:

> "And I tell you, you are Peter, and on this rock I will build my church, and the gates of hell shall not prevail against it." Matthew 16:18 (ESV)

It was not Peter who was the rock upon which the church was built. Rather it was the testimony, or witness which Peter gave when Jesus asked to find out who people were saying Jesus was. Peter spoke up and identified Jesus of Nazareth as the long-awaited Christ, the Messiah. On that testimony, the Christian Church was built.

Did Grampa know this? Did Grampa know Jesus? Perhaps not. Perhaps no one ever explained these or any other Christian teachings to him. Thus it begs the big question: was being the hard-working, honest, fatherly figure enough to get Grampa into the place called heaven when his earthly life was ended?

And what about me? Life did not seem fair to me with so many health issues. Who was God anyway, and why did He let these challenges shadow me?

I also vividly recall that night Grandpa visited me at Children's Memorial Hospital. Before he arrived, I looked on at a hospital bed near me. There was a child younger than I in the same kind of bed with the high bars. Standing next to the bed were the child's young parents. They were weeping as they looked at their child. It was the first time I can remember having experienced the emotion of compassion. It is an image which has stayed with me over the years. "Why is there this kind of sadness in this life?" I wondered.

Chapter 2
Hockey Icons and Tragedies

Fast-forward to the mid 60's. My sister and I were in for a surprise. Our parents remarried... to each other! Again, we were kept in the dark about everything. All we were told was Dad's job situation had changed and he would not have to labor far from home. Now we could all be a family together under the same roof. Grayslake, Illinois, a northern suburb of Chicago, became our home. The house which we were renting sat on a large corner lot. This was considered being in the country with acres and acres of rich Lake County farmland to the west of us.

At the inquisitive age of six years old, I was just starting to get to know my biological father. Robert "Bob" Amann grew up in the area. His Grandfather stowed away on a liner from Germany to the U.S. He was fleeing the army of the Kaiser, so the story goes. Others came too, and they were all farmers.

My Dad's dad was an accomplished poker player who carried around a little black book. The contents of that keepsake held the names of various people in town who owed him money from winning many backroom card games. Grampa Amann had mastered the game. He was once told his skills would carry him to victory at the national poker level. His response was short and definite, "I am good enough to know I am not good enough to play at the national games."

Our fraternal grandfather was also a part of the "Greatest Generation." He was in the Navy and fought in WWII as a gunner on a battleship. I once asked him, "How did you survive the Kamikaze planes that were crashing into the battle ships all around you?"

"I was extra careful shooting and made sure I didn't miss my targets on those days," he replied with a wry smile. Like so many other WWII vets, he just never talked about his war experience beyond that particular exchange.

Way back in the day, Dad and Grampa Amann had a falling out. It was a very serious argument, such that Dad left home as a teen. He lied about his age and joined the Marines at age seventeen. The Marines got his attention, literally on Day One. The new grunts were all lined up to get their shots when someone in front of him fell down and was having a seizure. The drill instructors screamed at the top of their lungs, "You will not stop to help this man! You will continue on!"

Dad's immediate thought was, "What am I doing here!"

He hung in there, though, and his military experience built him into a lifelong, gung-ho Marine. Many times I heard him say, "Semper Fi," the Marine slogan meaning "Always faithful," in Latin.

Dad seemed to be confident with himself, and he was popular with many people. He was always the life of the party having been gifted with a quick wit. But taking on the role of being a father was something very different; it was not in his comfort zone.

I, however, was learning what it was like to have a father. As an impressionable child I absorbed his life interests. One of those interests was cars. Dad liked all kinds of cars. Among his favorites were big Cadillacs. Dad had a 1959 black Eldorado with a white ragtop and brown leather interior. There were massive fins on the rear of the car and lots of chrome. The car was a gigantic living room on wheels. I can still recall bouncing around in the back seat, long before the era of seatbelts and car seats. (How did we ever survive without restraints?)

Dad enjoyed taking us out to buy root beer floats in his latest convertible, with the top down. Another destination was the outdoor theater. Both Dad and Mom were movie junkies so we saw several films at the outdoor theater including the original "Planet of the Apes" starring Charlton Heston, Roddy McDowall, and Kim Hunter. From the confines of the car, with the blaring speaker hanging on the driver-side window, we also saw the exciting "Bullitt." This was the famous movie with the super cool Steve McQueen and the greatest car-chase scene ever. Actors Robert Vaughn and a young Jacqueline Bisset were clearly upstaged by the green fastback Bullitt Mustang car McQueen ferociously drove into movie immortality.

Dad's car enthusiasm included auto racing at the local speedway where we watched race cars roar around the oval dirt track on Saturday nights under the lights. The race cars leaned on each other through the turns on the racing track. The rumbling engines, the smell of burning rubber, with dust and dirt swirling through the air in the heat of the night, are unforgettable.

We didn't talk much even though I wanted to. I had many questions about health and the whole church thing. Turns out Grampa Amann didn't go to church either. The noise levels were too high at the race track so talking would have been a challenge anyway.

One place where we communicated was in the universal language of laughter. The main source of the jocularity came from watching the "Classic 39" episodes of "The Honeymooners" with Jackie Gleason, Art Carney, Audrey Meadows, and Joyce Randolph. We watched them so many times that I still have some of those shows memorized line by line and laugh by laugh.

In addition to the car races, Dad watched football, baseball, and hockey. Looking back, there were times, or seasons in his life, where one sport would be more dominant than others. So, my Blackhawks hockey connection would continue.

In those days, I have to admit I enjoyed watching the campy Batman television show as much as I did the Blackhawks. The Caped-Crusader and his sidekick Robin chasing down eclectic criminals of all kinds, while speeding away in the world famous Batmobile, was a real hook. We still watched the Blackhawks on a black and white television. The screen was a much smaller one than Grampa Bruni had. However, technology had made a giant leap forward with remote control television. It was fun to endlessly push a button and change the TV channels without having to get off the couch. This amazing feat could be accomplished from anywhere in the living room.

At around the time of my parents' remarriage, Chicago Blackhawks hockey was right up there with football in Dad's eyes. Hockey was right up there with the public also. The National Hockey League jumped on the popularity and expanded from the "Original Six" teams to twelve teams.

One particular night our Dad came home with a major surprise. "How about this?" he asked. "The Blackhawks are sending Bobby Hull and Stan Mikita on a promotional tour to a nearby appliance store to meet the public and sign autographs. Do you guys want to go?"

Did we want to go?

Did we want to go and see Bobby Hull, a.k.a "The Golden Jet?" And "Stan the Man" Mikita? In the flesh? Mikita wore number 21 on his jersey and was often number one with the fans. Torn between him and Hull for the top spot of the hearts of fans, Stan Mikita would go on to play twenty-one seasons as a scrappy and consistent center for the Chicago Blackhawks. Mikita, who passed away in 2018, is still the all-time points leader for the team.

Mikita and Hull had major impacts on the game of hockey. Together they developed the curved hockey stick. This tinkering with the stick dramatically changed how the puck came off the stick on a shot. Their invention revolutionized the game. Imagine a shot from Hull's curved stick at more than 100 miles per hour! Stan Mikita was a pioneer in wearing a helmet during the hockey games. Eventually, rule changes in the NHL made the wearing of helmets mandatory across the league.

It was normal to have one career on one team, something almost unheard of today in the era of free-agency and savory financial contracts. Not only that, but you would be hard pressed to find a player signing autographs at an appliance store. But again, these were simpler times.

It was a bright Saturday afternoon when we arrived at the appliance store to get in line to take our turn to meet these larger-than-life sports icons sitting at a table amongst brand new washing machines and dryers, signing autographs. As we waited in line, we could see Bobby Hull and Stan Mikita and we could hear their voices. I remembered thinking, "Are we really going to meet these guys in person?" The line of fans was enthusiastic, but very long. It seemed like we would never get to the table. I was straining my neck to see around the throngs of people while Mom longingly eyed the brand new, bright white appliances. They were neatly set in rows with washing machines and dryers on one side, and refrigerators and stoves on the other.

We finally got to the front of the line. There was the Golden Jet with his famous smile, which was simultaneously charming and disarming. He signed his name on a piece of paper and shook my hand. Next up was Stan Mikita. Another smile, a handshake, an autograph, and then... my brief time with these heroes was over. I didn't say anything to either of them because I was too awestruck. There were simply no words! We went home with autographs and memories, but without any new appliances.

The years added on, one to another, while I closely followed the Blackhawks every season. As the turbulent decade of the

60's came to a close, the Vietnam War raged on. The war death tolls would be recounted on the evening news night after night after night. By contrast, there was also exciting news. Our nation sent shock waves around the globe by successfully landing two men on the moon. We did it in less than a decade by boldly and successfully answering the daunting challenge set by President Kennedy just a few years before.

At the same time, I began to wonder about faith and how that was supposed to fit into busy lives with so many distractions. We did go to church, but our church attendance took on a different pattern than we had in Chicago. Our family had moved to another suburb in the area, named Mundelein, after Catholic Cardinal George William Mundelein who died in 1939.

My sister and I would walk a couple of miles to attend church. Once there, we would sit in sections with other kids our age who also attended Sunday morning catechism classes. After church we would walk home, and along the way, one or both of our parents would pass by in the car. They were on their way to Catholic Mass at a different time. Sometimes Dad and Mom would go together, and other times they would attend at separate times.

Many years later I came to the conviction that one of the most powerful things a man can do is to lead his family into a Bible-believing and teaching church, sit down together and make a family commitment to worship and serve together through that house of worship.

For now though, I was thinking about God, and how my life had anything do with some of the fragments of the faith coming to me in bits and pieces. Some early awakenings came to me through my mom's advice, and also through tragedies going back to my first grade classroom at the St. Joseph's school in Libertyville, Illinois.

Mom was a hard worker and once gave me some counsel which directed my life as much as anything. I was about seven years old and was attending summer day camp. One day some kids from camp started picking on another boy my age. It did not seem right to me. I felt if I intervened, they would turn on me. As I considered the situation, justice welled-up inside me. Then I spoke up on his behalf and proved myself right... they left the other kid alone and they came for me.

Later that night I was lying in bed and quietly weeping, knowing what was in store for me the next day. My mother heard me. She came in and tenderly asked, "What's wrong, Terry? Why are you crying?"

When I told her what happened, I had a question for her. "Mom, did I do the right thing by standing up for the other kid?"

Her life altering response came in a gentle voice. "Yes, you did. You should always stand up for what's right. It may be hard, but it is the right thing to do."

Then came the tragedies. There were two boys from our first grade class who died. Coincidentally, both were named Mike. One of those boys died as a result of drowning; the other was killed in a fiery car accident along with the rest of his family. They had just purchased a Christmas tree and were driving home with the tree on top of the car when the crash occurred.

After each of these terrible events, our teacher, who was a stern elderly nun, told us these people were now in heaven with God. She said eventually all of us will die one day because everyone dies. Those young deaths, and her words, stuck with me.

I began to wonder about death. What does it mean to die? What happens? When and how am I going to die? I wasn't so sure I could count on the old adage, "It's always the other guy who dies." After all, people died every day – even the hockey players who seemed so much larger than life itself. One of my biggest questions was whether or not everyone automatically would go to heaven and be with God when they passed away.

The Bible makes it clear that death is inevitable for everyone:

> There is a time for everything, and a season for every activity under the heavens: a time to be born and a time to die. Ecclesiastes 3:1-2a (NIV)

> Just as people are destined to die once, and after that to face judgment. Hebrews 9:27 (NIV)

Even death has a season. What about the judgment part of death? What does that mean? All of these puzzling thoughts were unsettling to me. With death being certain and judgment to follow, I wondered, "What can be done?"

Chapter 3
Here Come the Hawks

In 1970, my hockey fortunes increased even more. My Dad asked me an incredible question. He said, "I can get tickets to the Blackhawks vs. the Boston Bruins playoff game for Sunday night. Do you want to go?"

Did I want to go?

Wow! My first National Hockey League game! And it wasn't just any game. This was an Eastern Division semi-finals playoff game. This was the last leg on the long journey to the coveted Stanley Cup Championship. The Stanley Cup dates way back to 1892 and is the oldest sports trophy contested for in all of North America.

On April 19[2], 1970, we drove from the safe haven of suburbia to the sketchy neighborhood of the Chicago Stadium, home of the Chicago Blackhawks and the Chicago Bulls. Michael Jordan and the amazing Bulls were still a twinkle in the eye of destiny to come. Since the Chicago Bulls were struggling so much, their game tickets were given away freely to try and get fans to their games. Not so for the Blackhawks hockey games. These were often sold out and hard to get.

---

[2] Many decades later, our youngest daughter was born on that day. Yes, she is also an avid Blackhawks fan.

Today, both the Blackhawks and Bulls play in The United Center, built in 1994. The Chicago Stadium, with its long and interesting history with the city, was torn down. The whole area around the United Center has been put through a significant regentrification process. But back then, it was more than a little unnerving to be walking around the neighborhood with burned-out buildings, dark alleys, and occasional gunfire.

We arrived safely at the now long-gone Chicago Stadium, also fondly called "The Old Barn." The Stadium was full of excitement as the fans streamed in. We watched what are called the warm-ups where the players practice before the game. This was a chance to get a good look at the players on the ice since they were not always going at full speed like they do in the game. Still to this day, I like to arrive at hockey games early enough to watch the warm-up skate.

After warm-ups, the players went back into the locker rooms and the Zamboni ice vehicle came out to smooth over the ice. When the Zamboni successfully completed its mission, the ice would be like a massive piece of sheer glass. Several minutes later, the players returned from their locker rooms to their respective benches. Now they were ready to go.

Next came the classic Chicago Blackhawks fan tradition: the singing of the National Anthem. The starting players line up on their defending blue lines, facing each other. The fans scream and cheer with unabashed patriotism as the song resonates throughout the rink. The cheering gets louder and louder as the anthem goes on. Trust me - you need to hear the emotion and excitement of the rendition of the National Anthem from a

Blackhawks game. There is nothing like it. Check it out on YouTube.

Finally, the big game was ready to begin. The Blackhawks were wearing red jerseys with the famous Blackhawk Indian patch. Their black pants boasted red and white piping down the side. The Boston Bruins wore the black jerseys. On the front of their uniforms was the big "B." They also had black hockey pants, but with yellow and white piping.

The Boston Bruins of course had their best player and one of the all-time greats, #4 Bobby Orr, at defense. Little did I know at the time, but Bobby Orr and I would cross paths several years later. Other Bruins hockey greats were there including Phil Esposito, Kenny Hodge, Wayne Cashman, Johnny Bucyk, Derek "Big Bad Bruin" Sanderson, Fred Stanfield, Eddie Westfall, and with Gerry Cheevers as their goaltender.

For the Blackhawks, we had Hull and Mikita along with other giants of hockey lore. Names like Eric Neterenko, Cliff Koroll, Jim Pappin, Jerry Pinder, Doug Mohns, Lou Angotti, Pit Martin, Bill White, Doug Jarret, Keith Magnuson, Dennis Hull, Gene Ubriaco, Paul Shmyr, and Byran Campbell. Also in the line-up was the famous goalie, #35 Tony Esposito. Tony had several nicknames, such as "Tony O" and "The Flopper," the latter given because of his unorthodox and game-changing style. "Espo" would use his whole body in whatever manner was needed to keep the puck out of the net. He was legendary "between the pipes."

I, of course, had my handheld transistor radio. This included the bulky headphones so I could hear Lloyd Pettit call the game. My Dad asked, "Are you going to listen to the game with that?"

"Oh, yeah!" I replied.

There was no way to really have a conversation with Dad, again, because of the noise levels in the Chicago Stadium. Every young boy wants to hear from his dad. There is a longing there for guidance and affirmation. My Dad did not have parenting tools passed down to him from his father and so the cycle continued. There is so much influence parents can have on their children, even in the most subtle ways. In that moment it was kind of okay though since I did not want to miss Lloyd Pettit call the hockey action. And I was not alone. You could see people all around the stands clutching their transistor radios with their headphones on, doing the very same thing.

The pace of the hockey game on the ice was much faster to watch in person than I expected. The crowd was totally into the game, offering "ooohs" and "aaaahs" at the "almosts" that took place. There was a powerful electricity in the air which gripped the fans. Everybody could sense it.

This was a huge game for Bruins player, Phil Esposito, known as "The Garbage Collector." This moniker was given to him because he would hang in front of the net waiting for a rebound he could tip into the net. He collected a whole lot of "garbage" that night. Phil got a "hat trick," scoring three goals in one game against his goalie brother, Tony. Ironically, Phil Esposito was a former Blackhawk until they traded him to the Bruins in a 1967 blockbuster deal.

Bobby Orr also had a big game having blocked three Blackhawks' shots that were headed for the goal line. One of those shots was a blast from #9 Bobby Hull. Orr also had an assist on Phil Esposito's second goal of the game. In the end, the Blackhawks fell 6-3 in a very rough and tumble contest. Even though the good guys lost, the score did not detract from the whole of the event. We still had the thrill of watching the Blackhawks score goals. Dennis Hull, Jim Pappin, and Stan Mikita all "lit the lamp," much to the wild roar of approval from the jam-packed crowd. The Chicago Stadium was definitely a place I had to visit again - and I did, many times over the years.

The Boston Bruins swept the Blackhawks in four games and then went on to sweep the St. Louis Blues four games in the finals to win the Stanley Cup. It was game four - played on May 10, 1970, in the famous Boston Garden - that will always be remembered. The game was tied 3-3, with the two teams going into sudden death overtime. And who else, but Bobby Orr, scored the winning goal. In the chaos of the moment, Orr was tripped up and sent flying through the air horizontally, while simultaneously lifting his arms in celebration. A photographer captured the moment and snapped the picture. It is a photo considered to be one of the greatest sports pics of all time.

A few years later, a family friend suggested we go watch the Blackhawks who were holding a team practice, open to the public, at a rink in Northbrook, Illinois. At the practice, my friend caught a puck that flew into the stands from the practice ice. He caught it mid-air. The markings on the puck proudly bore the famous hockey supplier "Gunzo's Sports" printed in orange on the black rubber disk.

After the practice was over and the players were leaving the rink, we noticed Bobby Hull standing in a phone booth talking on a pay phone. My friend dared me to go over and ask Hull to sign the puck. No problem. I went over, handed him the puck and a pen. "Mr. Hull, would you mind autographing this for me?" Hull was pleased to accommodate a fan, smiled, signed the puck on the orange part, and kept on talking on the phone.

We found out later that after Bobby Hull left the rink and was driving home, he surprised some fans along the way. Hull saw two young men hitchhiking that a friend of mine knew. Bobby Hull pulled over to give them a ride home. Can you imagine the shock those boys had when they realized who picked them up!

About a decade later, my friend gave me that autographed puck. Several years after that, I sold it for a nominal price, just because. At the moment of the transaction I watched in horror as the buyer rubbed Hull's autograph from the puck. He said, "I'm really just interested in Gunzo's name for my puck collection." Immediately I experienced seller's remorse.

The old Chicago Stadium with its tag line "Remember the Roar" is no more. Hockey greats from another era, transistor radios, pay phones, and hitch-hiking, are also memories fading into the annals of time. Yet, for me, there would be more excitement to come in my hockey world. Plus, my passion for the game just continued to grow.

The chase for the Stanley Cup, like any other trophy, has a season. After the prior season is finished, a new season gets underway. Over time people tend to forget who the previous champions were. Then another season and another season goes by. Pretty soon, players' names and their respective accomplishments become footnoted records, which are sure to be broken one day. Often, though, those same records are simply forgotten.

Given those facts of life, one might be tempted to ask some more thought-provoking questions: Is this what life is all about? In my case, did I need to become a professional hockey player to make the most of this limited life here on earth? Should I play hockey, make it to the National Hockey League with the Blackhawks, make lots of money, and live the American dream? Is that all there is? Thankfully, I realized the answer for me was that I did not have to become a hockey player. This was a relief because I was not good enough to make it even close to the NHL.

Eventually I found the answer to the more provocative question and to all questions. The playbook with all the answers is the Bible. In that sacred book we read about our very limited time here on earth:

> Yet you do not know what your life will be like tomorrow. You are *just* a vapor that appears for a little while and then vanishes away. James 4:14 (NASB)

Life is like a vapor. It sure does seem to be like it's here today and gone tomorrow. The concept of time and the experience of it are difficult to understand. In between the beginning and the end of life there is a desire for meaning, and for direction, and for fulfillment. Knowing there are all of these categories to address, we can easily become paralyzed in apathy or inaction due to fear of failure or lack of direction to follow.

In sports, the players always look to the coach. There is a coach for this life. He is God our Creator. Here is His instruction for how we are to forge ahead here on earth as found in God's playbook:

> The mind of man plans his way, But the Lord directs his steps. Proverbs 16:9 (NASB)

We have the Coach, and we have the playbook. It is left up to each of us to make the choice to live out the instructions and allow God to lead out. Unfortunately, too often we try to go it alone. When we do that, we just end up stumbling along through life and adding regrets to the journey. But the good news is that at any time we can turn to God and ask Him to direct our lives and He will. Just ask God, "Please Lord, direct my steps!"

When you do this, you will be along for the ride! Meaning and contentment come from a life lived through Him, so let God bless you with it. And most importantly, the Bible explains life and death and judgment and the answers to it all, as we shall see.

Chapter 4
School and More Hockey

I was now attending a public school for 5th through junior high grades at the small country schoolhouse in Rondout, Illinois. Rondout consists of the school, a few homes and a couple of businesses. It will always be known as the site of the Great Train Robbery of 1924.

There were the usual classes at Rondout School, including math. After all, math is a key building block of the universe. In arithmetic class, however, the numbers just never seemed to add up for me. Instead, I invested my class time doing artwork, unbeknownst to the teacher, although it became obvious to him by the time test results were in. I tuned out the scholastic instruction in order to draw cars, snowmobiles, and hockey players. My self-taught artistry grew immensely over the years. Even though some very fine early art pieces emerged from the numbers jumble, I was clearly left mathematically challenged. Chalk it up to another cross to bear.

Several years later I found out our math teacher from those years was also a Christian pastor. Unfortunately, he never let on to his Christian vocation in the public school. His faith instruction and wisdom might have helped me, and others, to understand some things about life and death and the in-between purposes of it all.

A highlight for me from those years was when we played floor hockey in gym class during the winter. It was always a very short season replaced by basketball, much to the displeasure of several of the guys. We just could not get enough of the floor hockey.

After grade school I attended Carmel Catholic High School in Mundelein, Illinois. As might be expected, I hung out with other guys who were interested in hockey. By this time, Blackhawk hockey was less important to my Dad than football. No matter though. Hockey was a part of me, as was football. Consequently, I played football all four years at that high school. This was the mid 70's, a time of rock 'n' roll, muscle cars, the bicentennial of our nation, and a collective reflection on the end of the Vietnam War years, which had scarred so many.

Our small cadre of like-minded teens talked a lot about hockey. Dave, the most colorful of us, was a Philadelphia Flyers fan. The Philadelphia Flyers had such luminaries as Bernie Parent, Bobby Clarke, and the notorious Dave "The Hammer" Schultz. So of course, we called our friend, Dave, "The Hammer." We could never understand why he rejected the Blackhawks.

Even though they hailed from the "City of Brotherly Love," the rest of us hated the Philadelphia Flyers. They were known by their bad-boy image as "The Broad Street Bullies." The Flyers were always more interested in fighting than playing hockey, racking up mountains of penalty minutes in just about every game. You may have heard the phrase, "I went to the fights and a hockey game broke out!" Well, that pretty much summed it up for the Philadelphia Flyers of that era. Mike, Steve, and I were Blackhawks fans, although Steve was less so. Chris was kind of ambivalent towards hockey. Interestingly enough, when the dust settled, Chris played on our hockey team that was to come, but Dave "The Hammer" did not.

After a couple of months of our freshman year, we started asking "What if?" questions about having our own high school hockey team. For the next two years, Mike and I made phone calls, talked with people, and worked toward putting a team together. In order to make the phone calls, we would ask other students to donate quarters for the pay phone in the school hallway.

Among the many things you need for a hockey team is a name. Our desire was to represent our school and be the Carmel Corsairs hockey team. We got the word from the high school administration that we would be able to use the official school team name as long as we could pull together a team in a legitimate league. These were great challenges put before us, but we were determined to follow through.

After two years of keeping hope alive, Mike and I persevered. We had players and a league and presented everything to the school administration. Surprisingly, they reversed their original position and said they would not sanction the use of the school name. Perhaps they thought we were just dreaming out loud and wanted to placate us two years before. Another possibility was because the team roster included students from other schools. In any event, now we needed a name for our nascent hockey team.

What seemed like a bad turn of events actually became an opportunity for us to have our favorite NHL team name.

However, making that choice became a source of heated discussion. Mike wanted the farm club name of the Montreal Canadians, who were then known as the Voyageurs. I, of course, wanted the Blackhawks to be our name. We argued intensely about this issue in the hallways between classes. Finally, we experienced the art of compromise. We agreed to use my hometown name of Libertyville and attach it to the Canadians farm team name. And so, our impossible dream was becoming a reality, right before our eyes. The Libertyville Voyageurs were preparing to take the ice as our high school hockey team was born.

In addition to putting together a hockey team, we kept our eyes on the Blackhawks, both on radio and television, and also in person. Mike and I went to numerous Chicago Blackhawks games. My Dad was not thrilled about us going so often. He reminded me of his displeasure on a couple of occasions. "You are wasting too much money on those Hawks games!" I always had one or two part-time jobs since the age of eleven. Therefore, I could afford the games. With a passion to see Blackhawks games in person, go and spend we did!

Seeing Blackhawks hockey was so important to Mike and me that once we even went on a double date to a game. Our dates didn't seem to appreciate the whole hockey experience in the loud Chicago Stadium. Maybe it was the affordable nosebleed seats that were too distracting for them. They were good sports about it all, but there were no second dates to a Blackhawks game.

Going from the pleasant confines of suburbia into the gritty city had its own challenges. First off, we had to decide who would be able to drive there. By our senior year, I had upgraded from a 1966 Ford Mustang to a 1967 Mercury Cougar. The drive time of an hour wasn't really the issue. What concerned us was going into that neighborhood with cars that might not always be dependable enough to get us back home. My Cougar was jacked up with wide rear tires and mag rims, which made it a nice target for theft. In other words, there might not even be a car there when the game let out.

There were some memorable trips into the Windy City on our way to the Chicago Stadium. Once when my windshield wipers stopped working as we drove down the Edens Expressway, I would reach out around the windshield from the driver's side of the car, and try and wipe the dirty snow and slush off, while Mike held the steering wheel at a cruising speed of 75 miles per hour. I would yell to Mike from outside the car with the wind blowing hard, "Mike, more to the right. No! Straighten it out! Easy Trigger..." We had to endure that precarious exercise a couple times on that particular trip. All the while we were keeping track of the time. After all, we had to get to the rink in time for the warm-up skate.

Another time, when it was my turn to drive, the Cougar was in the shop. So we borrowed Mom's car, a 1969 Plymouth Fury. We stopped at a nearby gas station to put gas in the car on the way. When we went to leave, the car wouldn't start. A gas station worker came out and poked around under the hood. He gave his professional diagnosis, "It's a bad starter. Hand me that hammer," he added, pointing to a greasy set of tools. He whacked the starter with the hammer several times - Wham! Wham! Wham! "Now try and start it."

With that, the car engine grumbled and started. "You boys better take that car straight over to the place you want to fix it 'cause it probably won't start again." Now there was no way Mike and I were going to miss the game. So off we went into the rough Chicago west side neighborhood at night.

Sure enough, after the game, the car wouldn't start. Neither one of us was carrying a hammer. Our hearts sank. This was not the place to be at that time of night. So there we were, in a questionable section of Chi-town, eons before the necessary convenience of cell phones. People were leaving the stadium and the parking lots, and before long, we were the sole car in the lot. Parking lot lights were being turned off all around us. We sat in the car like we were clinging to a life-raft in the middle of the ocean.

Somehow we found a way to call my Dad. I cannot recall how it all came together, but it did. Dad was not happy with me already for what he had said about spending money on the Hawks tickets. Now, here it was 10:45 PM and he had to drive into the city to come and get us, and have the car towed - somewhere. While we were glad to be 'rescued,' it was a very somber trip home. As usual, we did not talk much, but that night it was a good thing.

Mike and I had big plans for our hockey team. We were full of excitement for the near future. But it could all have come crashing down for me in a very horrific way. In the summer of 1976, I was still hitchhiking around because I did not get my first car until later that fall. There was no such thing as an Uber or Lyft driver in those days. On one particular weekday, I was thumbing my way westbound on Route 176. This is a main artery which goes through Libertyville to Mundelein in Illinois. I was on my way to Carmel High School. We had a liberal campus policy for students that allowed them to come and go depending on their classroom schedule.

So I stood there on the gravel shoulder with my thumb out as cars whizzed by. This form of travel, albeit somewhat dangerous, was also possible to cause me to be late for my classes. This seemed like it would be one of those days. Finally, a car pulled over. I checked my watch. There was still enough time to get to my class. As I opened the door the driver leaned over. His eyes seemed peculiar, almost bulging with intensity. He said, "Come on, get in." Stepping into the car, I did not bother with the seatbelt. That may have saved my life.

Then the driver asked, "Where ya' going?"

"Just down the road a couple of miles," I replied.

There was a little more small talk as we came into the Milwaukee Avenue and Route 176 intersection in Libertyville. The stop light was going from green… to yellow… to red. The driver started to slow down. Then suddenly, he swung his right arm around, leaned over, and grabbed my left leg. I immediately turned and looked directly at him. In the same motion, I thrust my right arm for the door handle and pulled it up. The split-second thought crossed my mind that if the door was locked, I was in serious trouble, but at least the seatbelt wasn't latched.

Mercifully, the door flew open. I jumped out into a full run from the car. I didn't look back. I just ran for two blocks and cut around a corner onto a side street. I was more disgusted by the whole event than scared. Plus now, I was going to be late for school. By the next day, I shrugged the whole incident off and was right back to my hitchhiking post.

Two years later John Wayne Gacy was arrested for the murder of thirty-three young boys, to which he pleaded guilty. The gory details of the case came out as twenty-nine of the bodies had been buried in the crawl space of his Norwood Park, Illinois home. All of his victims were killed at that location. He went on to death row and eventually was executed for his crimes by lethal injection in 1994.[3]

When the story broke, and his picture was plastered all over the news, I recognized him right away. John Wayne Gacy was the man who had picked me up in his car on my way to school. He was the one who suddenly grabbed my leg. I had looked pure evil in the face from just a few inches away and somehow had lived to tell about it. I also read in one of the news reports that he traveled along Route 176 on many occasions. Route 176 was almost always my launchpad. I guess when you are young and feeling immortal, a brush with potential death does not always get your attention as maybe it should. Besides, that was about number five in a series of maybe ten incidents over the course of my life that could have easily ended my time here on earth.

---

[3] Years later I was serving as a prison chaplain in jails, detention centers, prisons, and death row in the states of Illinois and Iowa, although our paths never crossed again. You can read about that ministry in my first book, Wednesdays with Barry.

It would be a few weeks after the Gacy arrest when I began to reconsider the thoughts I experienced in the first grade with the tragic deaths of those young boys. Such thoughts took me back to the big question – where would I have gone if I had died? Would I have gone to a place called heaven? Was I good enough to go there? Is being a 'good person' the standard to be able to get in? Or would I have gone to the place called hell? I wondered, were either of those places even real?

The answers to those challenging questions often take people by surprise. Yes, heaven and hell are real! But the biggest shocker is that *being a good person is not the ticket to heaven.* You can never be 'good enough' to get into heaven by all the 'good things' you do here on earth.

Stay tuned. More on that in chapter 9 of this book.

Chapter 5
The Mighty Voyageurs

The fall of 1976 finally arrived. Our team took to the ice for our first Voyageurs hockey practice. We had a couple of guys from our high school and some players (including my cousin Pete) from Libertyville High, the public high school just a few miles away on the same road, Route 176. There was a natural rivalry between CHS and LHS. Thankfully, we were able to set those emotions aside for the good of the Voyageur hockey team.

At that time, my father worked for The Independent Register, a local newspaper which promised the Libertyville Voyageurs newsprint coverage in the sports section of the paper. There was a catch, though. Dad informed me of what that meant. "We'll send a photographer to a game once or twice. Our sportswriter has all he can handle right now so we can't send a reporter to the rink. You will have to write the stories for the newspaper."

Thus, in addition to being a co-founder of the Libertyville Voyageurs and playing right wing for them, I would also be their sportswriter. I probably should have included sportswriter on my resume over the years, but I never did. There were several games where I was trying to focus on the action taking place while remembering who did what in the game. The only way to do it was to write fragments in my mind as the game went on and then get them to paper right afterwards. I would write out everything by hand and then peck away at the ancient black

Royal typewriter. Remember, there were no laptops or cell phones.

There was one incident where I tried to apply my active journalism skills for another important cause. I used my 'press credentials' to get into a girls swim team practice at Libertyville High School. The swim coach told my friend and me, "You are not allowed in the pool area during practice." I promptly told her I was a sportswriter for the Independent Register – which was kind of true. My self-appointed assignment was that I was interested in one of the young ladies on the team. We were able to get into the swim practice because the ruse worked perfectly. The relationship, however, did not.

Another major obstacle our hockey team had to confront was transportation. I was one of the few players on our team who owned a car. Consequently, we packed six people into my first car. It was an army green, 1966 Mustang. My Uncle Charlie had owned the car for a number of years. He passed it down to my cousin Pete, who in turn sold it to me. Now it had become the team bus of sorts.

The car had significant amounts of rust, especially underneath. In fact, the passenger side floorboard had a massive hole which opened onto the street. An old metal road sign was bent and fashioned to cover the hole. It wasn't even bolted down; it just lay over the hole. The foot pedal was long gone too, so you had to deftly push the metal stem with your foot in order to accelerate.

There were three people in the front with only two bucket seats. We had three people in the back seat made for none. We had all our equipment squeezed in and piled up on the open trunk. There were sticks and skates hanging out all over. We may have missed the boat by neglecting to contact Guinness World Records about that ride! To this day, I don't know how we were able to get everyone and everything into that Mustang according to the laws of physics.

Even though my first car had lots of rust, a metal road sign patching a hole in the floorboard, and too much weight, it somehow got us to all the games. Soon after the season ended, however, so did the transmission on my car. We simply burned it out. Amazingly, this was the only significant injury we had all hockey season.

Three young men saw the news articles about the Voyageurs hockey team forming and asked to join. Going on gut instinct, and trusting their verbal resumes, I told them they could play on the Voyageurs team. It was a risky move, but we needed some players to fill out the roster. This decision turned out to be one of my better calls in my life. Two of those three men came to be the best players in the league! And the third one was also a very good player. Together, those three additions would come to play a dramatic role in the hockey season ahead.

With time running out, we still had one more hurdle to overcome. We needed a hockey coach. That person had to be a volunteer because there surely wasn't any money around to pay them. Mike and I had asked several good prospects to coach our team but to no avail. We were ready to start without a coach if that was how it was going to be.

The games were to be played at a hockey rink in Waukegan, Illinois, which was also our practice arena. I will never forget how a remark at that very first hockey practice reverberated throughout the whole season...

As we took to the ice for our first practice, the chairman of the league was watching us. We didn't have a coach, nor did we have a whole lot of organization. In fact, I had never played ice hockey anywhere other than pick-up games at outdoor rinks, or when I would hand-shovel snow off of a pond near our house and play by myself. We were making it all up as we went along. The league chairman finally could no longer contain himself. Pointing at me, "Hey, you, come over here! Are you the one who started this team?" he asked menacingly.

"Yes sir, I did," I replied.

"Well, you guys are a disgrace!"

And with that declaration of opinion he turned and stormed off. I just stood there speechless for a few moments. Two years of toil and overcoming obstacles and this was our welcome into the world of ice hockey? Now I knew there was some kernel of truth in what he said. However, dreams which come from deep within give one a desire to press on, no matter what. Thus, press on we did. In the months to come, our fledgling hockey team would surprise the league chairman and everybody else, including us.

As the Libertyville Voyageur hockey season unfolded, it was obvious that two of our "walk-ons" were really good hockey players. One of them was Eli,[4] an African American. At that time, there were few African American hockey players, and very few players of his caliber, anywhere. Eli continually dominated the play in game after game, racking up many goals. In one game Eli had a three-goal hat trick, and in another he even scored four!

Unfortunately for Eli, and for us, he also led the team (and I think the league) in penalty minutes. Eli let his temper get the best of him. He would have a penalty called against him, argue with the ref, and then get more minutes added on while he skated toward the penalty box. You could hear a collective sigh from our teammates as we all thought, "Oh no, not again..." Since Eli never appeared in the big leagues, I can imagine that his anger might have held him back from ever going to 'The Show.' He clearly would have fit in well with the aggressive bad-boy Philadelphia Flyers.

The start of the hockey season brought on a special challenge which affected me directly. Our high school football coach, remembered for some of his famous sayings, like "Katie-Bar-the Door," and "Well, golly gee whiz," issued a decree at the beginning of the football season. He said, "No one will be allowed to play both football and hockey at the same time." This was, of course, exactly what I was planning to do. The end of the Carmel Corsairs football season overlapped the first month of the Libertyville Voyageurs hockey games. I would finish football practice, skip the shower, pick up everybody in the Mustang, and race over to the hockey rink. Once there, it was a quick dress into hockey equipment, practice, then change

---

[4] His name has been changed for this book.

47

again without a shower because there were none. In between all that, I was trying to keep up with schoolwork and a part-time job. No one else on the football team was playing both sports. I think our coach looked the other way since there were no negative consequences for me. I just had to get through those four weeks of intense extra-curricular activity.

The "Mighty Voyageurs," as my Dad called us, finally found a hockey coach along the way. We were starting to come together as a team. It happened because we stayed focused and we persevered through many obstacles.

Life takes many turns over the years. Some of those curves are tough to take. It was hard for Mike and me as we had roadblocks pop up and make plans difficult. You get through them and you finally accomplish what you are trying to do. Sometimes that end goal isn't all that you thought it would be. So you question, "Is this it? Is this as good as it gets?" In God's playbook, the Apostle Paul explains:

> And not only that, but we also boast in our sufferings, knowing that suffering produces endurance, and endurance produces character, and character produces hope, and hope does not disappoint us, because God's love has been poured into our hearts through the Holy Spirit that has been given to us.
> Romans 5:3-5 (NRSV)

Paul is telling us that the person who has put their trust in Jesus will still have trials and tribulations in this world, but they are never without hope. When you have given your life over to Him, and have decided to let God direct your steps, you come to learn that He is using all of the challenges you face. Each one of these trials and tribulations is an opportunity for God to build your character, and to make you more like Him.

God does it all. It is amazing what God has done for us through His Son Jesus. He sent Jesus to live among us and to die on the cross for us. When Jesus left this world, God sent the Holy Spirit of God, the third person of what is known as the Trinity of God: Father, Son, and Holy Spirit. The Holy Spirit comes to live inside of each believer (2 Timothy 1:14). The Holy Spirit acts as a helper and a counselor, which means we always have help if and when we need it (John 14:16, 26). People may let us down from time to time, but God never will!

I did not realize that Divine assistance was available back when we were slugging through the various difficult tasks to put a hockey team together. But what I did come to know later was how God was using those events in my life to build my character. I was learning the timeless value of perseverance.

Chapter 6
Game On!

We had a very wild and amazing hockey season. There were fights, there were goals, and there were many victories. When it was all said and done, we simply shocked everybody. Our overall record was 10-4-1. We held first place throughout the season, only to finish in second place due to a loss to the Bulldogs right at the end of the regular season schedule.

The Bulldogs were the team coached by none other than, the league chairman. It all happened in a tight game with the final score 5-4 in favor of the Bulldogs. Eli, ever the clutch player, scored late in the third period of the game. However, we just couldn't get that tying goal to even the score. They beat us, but not as handily as the chairman would have suspected. As painful as this particular loss was for us, the story does not end with that game.

When the playoffs came down to the final Championship game, we were in it! Adding to the drama, the Voyageurs were once again pitted against the Bulldogs. Despite the glory of the moment, this presented a tremendous personal heartache for me. The congenital urinary tract birth defect, which required so many surgeries over the course of my life, was active. In fact, in 1976 alone, I had undergone four of those surgeries. The problem was that my fourth surgery was scheduled over the Championship game timeframe. The surgery could not be postponed.

My life-long desire of playing hockey on a hockey team and going all the way to the finals would thus be crushed by events beyond my control. So, on the night of the championship game, I lay in a bed at Children's Memorial Hospital in Chicago, recovering from surgery. At the time, I broke some records at the hospital. With each successive surgery I had as a teen, I became the oldest 'child' to have a procedure there. Each time the doctor would ask me if I wanted to have the next surgery at the Children's Hospital. My answer was always the same - "Yes" - since I knew the place so well. The female nurses seemed to enjoy conversation with a teen, for a change. In return, I enjoyed their special attention.

Some fifty-five miles away from the ice rink, I lay in my small hospital bed anxiously awaiting news about the game. "Were the guys ready to get at it?" I wondered. It was excruciating to watch the hours tick by so slowly. There was one little light keeping my hospital room lit and the television was off. As I lay there, I played over in my mind what I thought might be happening. Then I began to feel very sad about the fact that another surgery had invaded my life. The timing for this medical adventure could not have been any worse.

Finally, my father arrived. He burst in through the door with a huge smile on his face, and proudly proclaimed, "The Mighty Voyageurs did it! You guys are champions! You guys won 3-2! It was a sudden-death overtime win!"

The news of a fantastic win to cap off a Cinderella season brought tears to my eyes. Wow! I couldn't wait to hear all the details. The moment was made even more special because we were communicating in such a powerful way. Dad and I were speaking the same language. Sports can do that for people.

I listened intently to every word as my Dad recapped the miraculous win. Our Voyageurs were down 2-0 with only seventy seconds left to play in the game. We scored a goal, which put the Bulldogs back on their heels making it a nail-biter of 2-1. Just a few seconds later it was none other than Eli who blasted a slap shot into the net to tie up the game. The final buzzer for regulation sounded. This game was going into sudden death overtime.

Glory upon glory as Eli wasn't finished yet. At the 8:42 mark of the first overtime period Eli scored a goal – but the referee had just raised his arm to call a penalty against us. Therefore, the goal was not allowed. How much more drama do you need to get the blood going! Not only was the goal disallowed but we had to play short-handed while our player sat in the penalty box for two minutes.

We killed off the penalty. The game went on. Then, with just a few seconds left on the clock in the first overtime period, it happened. Once again, Eli was destined for greatness. He and the two other guys I had added to our roster, solely on gut instinct back at the beginning of the season, came roaring up ice. They quickly passed the puck back and forth, eluding the defense. The final pass came to Eli. He was ready and could smell victory. Eli wound up and took a blistering slap shot on goal. There was a split-second to wait. Then the red light behind the net came on signifying a goal! Eli put the game winner past the Bulldogs' goalie to beat him, the buzzer, and the Bulldogs. Whatever injustice I was feeling for having to have another surgery was lost in all the excitement of the game. We did the seemingly impossible.

The postscript to that unforgettable hockey season had some noteworthy twists. First, I saw the league commissioner soon after getting out of the hospital. I looked him right in the eye and said, "I guess we aren't such a disgrace anymore." Once again, he turned and walked away from me.

The league chairman had no response, yet apparently, he had the last word. The rumor was that his son's team got trophies for winning the division, and the truth was we never received trophies for winning the Championship. A decade later, my wife bought me a statue of a hockey player we had spotted in a store in New Jersey. In a strange connection, that bronze hockey player was wearing my college football number 29. (I had played one year of football for the University of South Dakota Coyotes.) "Now," she said, "you have your trophy."

Justice delayed is still justice deserved.

Trophies are a funny thing. They are desirable and there is a great satisfaction in competing for them. Yet, the realities of trophies are that you need to keep them, store them, dust them, and relocate them when you move. Then as the years go by people don't really seem to notice them, or care about them, because there are other winners and other distractions and so on.

And then there was our high school. They got on board for the spring hockey season. There was a new team in the league called The Carmel Corsairs. Another life lesson learned:

everyone loves a winner. So there it was. The Libertyville Voyageurs won it all in our maiden season. Then we were gone. Perhaps it is fitting to have one season like ours and then close the books. After all, could any season ever be as extraordinary as this?

Well the answer is yes. Just a few shorts years later, the world of sports witnessed the 'Miracle on Ice' with the 1980 USA Hockey Team. They were the extreme underdogs to the always feared Russian Hockey Team. Somehow, they pulled it off and lifted our country at the same time. By then, the "Mighty Voyageurs" had faded into a small fleeting moment of hockey history.

Our solo hockey season was truly exciting and miraculous, but it was still only a small segment of my life. I have learned over the years that the Christian life, while often very challenging, is also exciting and miraculous. In fact, miracles are God's specialty.

For example, in the Biblical story of the Exodus, Moses is leading Israel out of slavery in Egypt. Pharaoh and his army are hot on their heels. Now comes a tremendous miracle recorded in the Old Testament of the Bible:

> Then Moses raised his hand over the sea, and the LORD opened up a path through the water with a strong east wind. The wind blew all that night, turning the seabed into dry land. So the people of Israel walked through the middle

> of the sea on dry ground, with
> walls of water on each side!
> Exodus 14:21-22 (NLT)

Pharaoh and his army went in after them and the waters engulfed them, allowing the Israelites to escape.

The New Testament also tells us about many fascinating miracles. Here is one that again involves water. Jesus was at a wedding in Cana, and the wine, which was so important to the celebration, ran out. Jesus was summoned to solve the dilemma:

> Standing nearby were six stone water jars, used for Jewish ceremonial washing. Each could hold twenty to thirty gallons. Jesus told the servants, "Fill the jars with water." When the jars had been filled, He said, "Now dip some out, and take it to the master of ceremonies." So the servants followed His instructions. When the master of ceremonies tasted the water that was now wine, not knowing where it had come from (though, of course, the servants knew), he called the bridegroom over. "A host always serves the best wine first," he said. "Then, when everyone has had a lot to drink, he brings out

the less expensive wine. But you have kept the best until now!" This miraculous sign at Cana in Galilee was the first time Jesus revealed His glory. And His disciples believed in him. John 2:6-11 (NLT)

Our one and only hockey season is a great memory and was certainly worth all that we put into it. However, looking back now, it was just a moment in time. By contrast, the Christian life is the season that never ends. As I said before, the Christian life can be difficult at times, but it is definitely worth it – so miraculous and exciting along the way. If you want to talk about "Game On," witness somebody who comes to salvation in Christ. There is nothing in this life more miraculous or more beautiful than that.

Chapter 7
Hanging with Hockey Greats

Amazing things can happen in this world every once in a while. Our only hockey season was one of those. Then along came more events to add to the excitement.

During our senior year in high school, Mike got involved with a charity run by none other than Stan Mikita. It was a hockey camp for people who were blind. For one of their events, Stan Mikita brought in Bobby Orr to headline a charity game for them. The gala was being held at a local practice arena.

The Boston Bruins' Bobby Orr is considered to be the best defenseman and all-around best player to have ever seen hockey action in the National Hockey League. Bobby Orr also happened to be my third favorite hockey player, behind Stan Mikita and Bobby Hull. My friend and hockey team co-founder, Mike, called me on the phone and asked a thrilling question. "Hey, do want to meet Stan Mikita and Bobby Orr?"

Did I want to meet Stan Mikita and Bobby Orr?

"Really! – how's that gonna' happen?" I exclaimed with great wonder. The plan was for me to go to the charity game and afterwards go into the locker room and meet these hockey giants.

Incredible as it sounds Bobby Orr was now a Chicago Blackhawk. He had a bad knee, and the Hawks were willing to take a chance on him while the Bruins were not. He would only play twenty-six games for Chicago before it was just too much for that knee and Orr would finally have to retire.

Sure enough, post-game, I walked into the locker room and was introduced to Stan Mikita. Here it was, over a decade since I had gotten his autograph back at the appliance store. We spoke for a few moments and then it was on over to Bobby Orr who was sitting on a bench up against the wall. You could sense he just enjoyed everything about the game of hockey, including the camaraderie of the locker room. Orr had a great smile and really seemed to enjoy the time as we exchanged pleasantries. Both Mikita and Orr were very gracious, even though it was late and they both had been playing hockey for a couple of hours and had been assisting others on the ice.

As awesome as this memorable evening was, the story gets even crazier from here. Fast-forward just about six hours. I had to get up early to go to one of my part-time jobs where I was a caddy at the fashionable Knollwood Country Club in Lake Forest, Illinois. I had started as a caddy in the summer after 6th grade. There was a bully from my grade school who was also a caddy there. He had made his presence known with rancorous laughter, "You will caddy for one day! Today only! You can't handle this work. You will go home and never come back."

The first golf bag was almost as big as me so he might have been on to something. However, all he did was motivate me to press on. So for the next several summers I would be up early and be one of the first caddies to get to the golf course. Within two years I was carrying "doubles." This means I would carry two golf bags at the same time. A "loop" was eighteen holes of golf. As soon as the loop was finished, I would collect my pay and tips, and then go back out for another loop of eighteen holes with doubles. Each loop would take about five and a half hours. There were also times I would even go out with a single bag for another nine holes after having completed thirty-six holes. These were typically twelve to thirteen-hour days. I often had to skip lunch in order to get right back to it. The bully was right about one thing: work on the golf course was grueling.

On this particular day, my cousin and fellow Libertyville Voyageur, Pete, arrived at the golf course before I did. He was asked to caddy in a foursome with some special guests. He wasn't interested, though, because he preferred to work in the caddy shack. It was much cooler in there. Being a worker in the caddy shack was also much better on your back and neck. Carrying those heavy golf bags up and down the course took its physical toll on the human body. No doubt a later football injury to my back was related to that caddy job. Additionally, a car accident, followed by an elevator accident, would compound the original stress on my back and neck.

Cousin Pete and I noticed a pattern about the abilities, or lack thereof, of golfers. The worse the golfer was, the heavier the golf bag they had. We called those burdensome bags "trunks." We called the low tippers "cheap shots." People with heavy trunks were often cheap shots also. Whenever they would come around, the caddies would scatter so as not to be told by the caddie master they had to take that loop. Always the hustler, I just took whatever came.

Many hockey players are also golfers. This would not be the case for me. I walked too many miles up and down the fairway, rough, and green grasses of the Knollwood Country Club while in bare feet. It was usually hot, and the bags were heavy.

The caddy master was the one to dole out the loops. He saw me coming up. I had been there for six golf seasons and had seniority over the other caddies. The caddy master told me he had a special loop. Three Knollwood members had special guests with them and they needed to be treated very well.

"Who are the guests?" I asked.

The caddy master turned and pointed, "Over there."

I turned around and just about passed out on the ground. There was Bobby Orr, sometimes known as "Number 4," referring to the number on his Boston and Chicago hockey jerseys. Bobby Orr came over to meet me. He put his hand out to shake mine, but then a quizzical look erupted on his face. "Hey, don't I know you from somewhere?" he asked. We laughed a roar of approval at the fact that we had just met a few hours previously at the charity hockey game.[5]

The other special guest was the Blackhawks own defenseman, Keith Magnuson. He and Chicago Blackhawk Cliff Koroll, who played wing, had attended the University of Denver together. One day they called up the Blackhawks organization

---

[5] Years later, I would meet the famous actor, James Earl Jones, in the same kind of weird circumstances – twice in less than 24 hours.

and asked for a tryout. Both men went on to play their whole careers in Chicago.

Magnuson was driving a golf cart, but not playing golf because he had a broken leg. Another local man of wealth, whose name I cannot remember, filled out the golf foursome. Here was the special loop my cousin Pete had turned down.

After everyone teed off on the first hole, Orr and I walked down the fairway together. He laughed when I ditched my shoes (as usual) once we got out of sight of the caddy master. Bare feet were against the rules, but the warm cut grass crunching against my feet brought relief from the miles of walking to be done on the course. Except, of course, when a golfer sliced the ball into the land of the rough or the wilds of the forest.

I always wore my trademark, white with blue lettering Carmel High School football practice jersey. There were similarities between the burdens of caddying and football practice: the hot sun, a lack of drinking water, and pressing on. My jersey was cut off at the shoulders to be sleeveless, and also at the waist above my belly button. Well-worn denim shorts with frayed ends completed the ensemble. It was quite a contrast with the golfers who always wore expensive threads to match the sport of golf. As we settled in, Bobby Orr asked me, "So Terry, do you like hockey?"

My first thought was, "Somebody, please pinch me. Is this really happening?"

For the next five and a half hours, four men walking (and a man in a cart) played golf. They laughed a lot, smoked big cigars, drank beer, laughed some more. They also bet big money at each hole. For my part, as an anonymous caddy, I strolled through the fields of ambrosia in hockey heaven. And I wasn't the least bitter about how Bobby Orr helped the Bruins stop the Blackhawks back in the 1970 semi-finals. In fact, I didn't even mention it.

At the final hole, as if in a fairy tale, it was all over. I could appreciate the mindset of Cinderella when the clock struck midnight. I have heard it said before that "thanks are not appreciated without cash." On this amazing day, however, I would have gladly worked the loop for free. Yet, Bobby Orr came by to thank me, and then tipped me $50.00 when a typical 'good tip' in those days would have been $15.00 per golfer. The other golfers also passed along some financial thanks to add to the thrill of it all.

I did not have the opportunity to meet Magnuson nor Orr again. Tragically, several years later, Keith Magnuson was killed in a car accident on his way to an alumni players meeting. His Blackhawk #3 jersey was retired, and proudly hangs from the rafters at the United Center in Chicago. I can still see "Maggie," as he was sometimes called, with a big cigar leaning back on the golf cart. His leg was in a cast and stretched out over the front of the cart. All the while he affectionately teased the hockey great, Bobby Orr.

Death can be so sudden and come upon us without warning. We make plans for tomorrow and the next day as if we are definitely going to have this time here on earth. When someone we know dies, we give pause and remind ourselves, even if just for a few moments, there are no guarantees for a tomorrow. When we die, we take one giant leap into a forever place called eternity. We all have an appointment with death. None of us will miss that rendezvous.

Since death is inevitable, we all have a decision to make – the decision which determines where we will spend eternity. Are we going to follow Jesus and have our sin debt removed, or are we going to choose to go our own way and die in our sins? God's love is so enormous that He gives us a free will to choose our destiny. God could have made robots. Instead He offers us eternal life, where we can come to have an intimate relationship with Him.

Think of it this way. Four decades ago, I proposed to my wife, Susan. I asked her, "Will you marry me?" I did not force her to marry me. If I had, I would never know if she really loved me. By giving her the choice, she knew she loved me, and I knew she loved me.

In the Biblical account, after Moses led the Israelites out of captivity, he died, and Joshua became the new leader of the Jews. Joshua reminded the people of all that God had done for them to deliver them from Egypt:

> ...Choose this day whom you will serve, whether the gods your fathers served in the region beyond the River, or the gods of the Amorites in whose land you dwell. But as for me

and my house, we will serve
the LORD. Joshua 24:15 (ESV)

As we consider what God has done for us through His only Son Jesus, we are faced with the most important question this side of heaven: will we choose to turn to God in faith? As for me, Terry Amann, and my household, we will serve the Lord. Will you?

At some point, each of us will stand before the Lord in judgment and the Bible is clear that no sin is allowed in heaven. I have heard it wisely said there will only be two kinds of people: those who are trusting in their good works, foolishly trying to make their sins go away; and those whose sins are covered by the sacrificial blood of Jesus Christ. It is only the second group which will be welcomed into the heavenly gates. I have traveled to several countries in order to share this truth. I like to ask people what might be called The Million Dollar Question: "Where will you go when you die?"

Dear reader, where will you go?

Chapter 8
Madison Street

Susan and I met at college at the University of South Dakota (USD) in Vermillion, South Dakota. Her family had recently moved to Aberdeen in the northern part of the state. I had decided I needed a dramatic change of scenery from my hometown roots and Vermillion was it.

Susan did not know much about hockey, but she took to it over time. Together we watched the incredible 1980 U.S. Hockey Team defeat the Russians. We watched that momentous game on a black and white television. It was much smaller than Grampa's old Zenith, and even smaller than the TV my parents had back in the 60's. Ten months later we would be married.

I played football my freshman year as a USD Coyote. The reality of college football is that you get hurt on every play. The question is always how bad is the hurt? The day after a game, I would typically be in my dorm room laying on the Ma Barker style couch my roommate and I procured from an abandoned farmhouse. I could hardly move because all areas of my body were in pain. I would watch the Chicago Bears football game on TV as if to be in sympathy with those players, if nothing else. After one season, it seemed like hitting the books rather than the gridiron might be a better long-term plan. Not only was my body battered but my grades were not looking very good either.

A few times at the local outdoor ice rink, I was able to hone my hockey skills with another hockey fan. We would skate while imagining great crowds were watching the big game. In reality though, there was no one else out there. Our only companion was the bitter cold wind of a South Dakota winter. And there wasn't really a way to follow the Chicago Blackhawks from Vermillion, South Dakota. For the first time in my life, hockey was taking somewhat of a backseat, in this case to college life and to Susan.

Love blossomed and we decided to get married over Christmas break in 1980. Susan and I enjoyed sitting by each other as husband and wife during our 1981 graduation ceremony. Unfortunately for us, and for the rest of the "Class of '81," the economy was in a deep recession. My Dad remarked that day, "The only people who are going to get jobs in this economy are the nurses!"

We decided our best hope of finding employment was to head back to the big city of Chicago. We loaded up our few worldly possessions into a U-Haul. We pulled that trailer with a red, 1973 AMC Gremlin X which boasted a manual transmission. Wouldn't you know that car had racing stripes on both sides that everyone said looked like hockey sticks. We left Vermillion ready to tackle the world. We were young marrieds, broke, owning little in the way of material things, yet full of hope.

After about five years of long hours and hard work, Susan and I were both doing very well in corporate America. She worked for a couple of places before she landed a position with the Sara Lee Corporation. Their world headquarters was right in Chicago, downtown on Madison Street. Just a little farther south on Madison was the Chicago Mercantile Exchange, where I was a commodities trader. One more block south was our luxury apartment at Presidential Towers. Several blocks further south was the old Chicago Stadium. That strip on Madison Street had everything; it was our life. And once again, the Blackhawks were front and center.

In the corporate arena, upper management usually has many perks. Sara Lee Corporation was no different. They had four seats for every Blackhawks home game. These were corner seats about eight rows up from the ice. Several times a year, upper management could not use the tickets so Susan would be given the option to have them. She would call me at work. "I have the tickets for the game tonight if we want them."

We always wanted them.

Just like that, we would find two other people to go with us and head to the Chicago Stadium, arriving in the nick of time to catch the warm-ups. Then came the National Anthem and the loud patriotic cries of the crowd. By then hockey greats of a generation were gone and it was a new breed of players. They played the game faster. They wore helmets. Still, the thrill was as awesome as ever.

A side note about the free tickets. I was never a basketball fan per se. Sara Lee also had four tickets for Chicago Bulls games. The tickets were made available to Susan late one afternoon. She called me on the phone at work. "Do you want the Bulls tickets?"

"Not really. It's been a tough day in the markets. Besides, it's basketball. Let them go."

So Susan said no to the tickets. A couple of days later I thought about that game and asked her, "Hey Susan, were those Bulls tickets the same as the Blackhawks game seats? Where were they?"

"No. Actually they were behind the Bulls bench," she said nonchalantly.

"What? You mean… like… right behind the bench…? The row directly behind Michael Jordan and the rest of the Chicago Bulls team?"

"Well yeah. You said you didn't want them."

Nice call, Coach. The Bulls tickets were never offered to us again, and consequently, we never saw "Air Jordan" play hoops in person. Not once.

In addition to making lots of money and going to Blackhawks games, I felt the urge to play hockey again. I signed up to play some hockey in an adult league. Ice time in Chicago was so expensive that we would play our games sometimes at 1:00 or 2:00 a.m. in the morning. My wife chose not to attend the games for obvious reasons. No other fans did either.

Life was all good and comfortable. And then something dramatic happened that changed everything. I was about to learn exactly what Jesus meant when He said these compelling words:

...If anyone wants to come with Me, he must deny himself, take up his cross, and follow Me. For whoever wants to save his life will lose it, but whoever loses his life because of Me will find it. What will it benefit a man if he gains the whole world yet loses his life? Or what will a man give in exchange for his life? Matthew 16:24-26 (HCSB)

Chapter 9
Game Off and the Victory of Faith

At some point it all comes to a close. There are just so many hockey games you can play. The late Gordie Howe, known reverently as "Mr. Hockey," played the game for an unheard of thirty-one seasons – twenty-five in the National Hockey League with the Detroit Red Wings, and six in the now defunct, World Hockey Association. It seemed like he could play forever. But like everyone else, Gordie Howe was mortal after all.

Having been inspired by Gordie Howe, I continue to play in adult hockey leagues at the age of 61. I've still got game and I plan to skate on. My personal stats have not caught up to those of Mikita, Hull, Orr, nor Howe. In fact, I didn't even get a hat trick (three goals in one game) until just two years ago. There were many games where I had two goals, and in a bid to get the hat trick, I would hit the goal post instead of scoring that elusive third goal.

In this particular game the clock showed just 45 seconds left to play. My wife and youngest daughter were watching in the stands. Rachel said to her Mom, "Dad would have to score in the next few seconds if he is going to get a hat trick." My teammate, Teague, took the face-off and got the puck behind the net. From there he passed it out to me and "Wham!" The puck slid past the goalie underneath his right skate and into the net. Finally, after so many years, I did it! Our daughter got her wish.

Another interesting personal stat is that I have never been in the penalty box. There was one game where I was called for fighting, but that was after time ran out on the clock and the game. Consequently, I never had to sit in the "sin-bin" as it is sometimes known for an on-ice infraction.

It remains to be seen whether I will ever play in a championship final game. Still, one day I will have to say, "Game off." It will be a time when I have to hang the skates up for good. What then? Players retire, and then eventually they pass away. In fact, everyone does. As we know with 100% certainty, 100% of people die.

Records are forgotten even though they are stored. The winner of the Stanley Cup Championship finishes the season in the middle of June. They return to hockey camp in September with everyone wanting to know who is going to win the next Stanley Cup. In other words, "What have you done for me lately?"

I began to think more about God and about my own life and eternal destiny. One particular day in college, while we were dating, Susan said to me, "You really don't know much about the Bible." This was a true statement. Her antidote to that issue was for me to sign up for a Bible class on the New Testament. I had to purchase a Good News Bible, which is a simpler translation, and then show up for class. There wasn't much spark in the instruction, and I was more concerned about a grade than I was about coming away with something spiritual.

Ten years later, after a decade of church attendance together as a married couple, the topic came up again. Susan keenly noted, "You still don't know much about the Bible." Again, she was correct. But this time I decided to do something about it. Hence, I pulled out the Good News Bible from my college days. I began with the Gospel of Matthew and read carefully and consistently. It did not take long before I would look forward to my next read. The general Bible stories I knew from prior years were now being filled in. The questions I had about life and death, meaning and purpose, and even church attendance were being answered for me as the Holy Spirit of God helped me to understand the Bible.

I was beginning to grasp who and what the main character was about. He is Jesus of Nazareth, who claims to be sent by God, and claims to be God. As I read more and more of the Scriptures, I came away with only two possibilities. Either Jesus is who He says He is, or He is a crazy man. He certainly did not act like a crazy man. In fact, He seemed to be very wise and compassionate.

Soon it became absolutely clear to me that Jesus is who He claimed to be. He is both the Son of God and He is God. With that realization, my life was forever changed and my goals - pun intended - were also permanently altered. I became a Born-Again Christian. I put my faith and trust in Jesus as my Savior.

Allow me to share with you what foundational Biblical principles I learned about the Christian faith.

God loves us so much that He made us "fearfully and wonderfully." In fact, God made us in His very image! God did not create bots. Rather, in His love, He gave us each a free will to choose to love Him back, or not. He invites each of us with open and loving arms, but He does not force us to know Him.

Yet, we choose to reject God through our rebellion and sin. When sin first came into the world (in the Garden of Eden), it brought the curse of death with it. Thus we have an inherited sin nature and a powerful desire to sin. When we sin, we are going against God's laws and we are separating ourselves from Him.

God desires us to know Him. In order to know Him, we must develop a relationship with His Son, Jesus Christ. It is that personal relationship with Jesus which takes away our sins and opens wide the gates of heaven. We need to come to know Jesus.

The problem is that we all think we are a 'good person' or at least good enough because we can point to way worse people. Yet God's standard of what it means to be 'good' is very different from ours. Scripture tells us:

> For *all* have sinned and
> fall short of the glory of
> God. Romans 3:23 (NASB)

None of us is a good enough person to get into heaven on our own merit. You can easily see that by asking yourself honestly, "Have I ever told a lie? Have I ever looked lustfully at someone? Have I ever used a swear word? Have I ever stolen anything?" If you are like me, your honest answers reveal that you are a lying, lustful, blaspheming, thief – all of which are sins that go against God. Again, if you are honestly examining yourself, you will recognize the need for a Savior.

God took the initiative and sent His Son, Jesus, into the world to save us from our sins. When Jesus came to the earth, He gave a brief, but urgent message of salvation:

> The kingdom of God is at hand; repent and believe in the gospel. Mark 1:15 (NASB)

To repent means to make a conscious effort to turn away from sin. If we turn away from something, then we have to turn toward something else. The answer is to turn to God in faith, and we put our trust in Jesus. The Bible holds this eternal promise:

> Truly, truly, I say to you, he who hears My word, and believes in Him Who sent Me, has eternal life, and does not come into judgment, but has passed out of death into life. John 5:24 (NASB)

There is judgment because God is just. Yet God desires *us* to reject sins and enter into His loving arms. When we repent by being truly sorry for our sins, and then we ask Jesus to be our Savior, His Holy Spirit comes and lives inside of us. When that happens, our sins are wiped away and forgotten by God. It does not matter how bad our sins might have been; God forgets them all! At that moment we become a "Born-Again" Christian.

Jesus specifically said that unless a person is Born Again, they cannot see the Kingdom of God (John 3:3).

Hockey is not like faith. In order to play hockey, or any sport, it takes a lot of work called practice, practice, practice. Not so for being Born Again to have your sins washed away! Since we are all sinners, no amount of practice at being good will ever cut it. So just going to church will not get us into heaven. Church attendance is a good thing, and we are called to do it in the Bible. However, it is not enough to get us into heaven, in the same way that nothing else we might do can get us into heaven, either.

Doing 'good works' or being a 'good person' will not get you into heaven!

Jesus Christ did all the work that needs to be done for you to be saved. Jesus did that by going to the cross for you, as a perfect sacrifice for your sins. God demands a payment for each and every sin. This means we all have a huge sin debt which must be paid. The required payment for the sin debt is perfection. We all sin and therefore, are not perfect, but Jesus is perfect. He never sinned--not even one time. In all my years of hockey, I never sat in the penalty box. It's not because I never committed a penalty; it's because I never got caught. Jesus however, never sinned.

Because Jesus never sinned, His death was the perfect, acceptable sacrifice to God for our sins. Think about it... We sinned. Jesus never did, but He went to the cross to pay our sin debt. He died the death we should have died. Jesus took our place. Jesus paid the price that only He could pay:

> Jesus said to him (Thomas), "I am the way, the truth, and the life. No one comes to the Father except through Me." John 14:6 (NKJV)

Then Jesus proved to be the all-time Champion, by being raised up from the dead three days later, just as He said He would. His resurrection from the dead is a guarantee to all people who believe in Him. The guarantee is victory over sin and death. This glorious victory showers all believers with eternal life in heaven. In heaven, there is no sin and there is no death. God's promise for believers is summed up here:

> For the wages of sin is death, but the free gift of God is eternal life in Christ Jesus our Lord. Romans 6:23 (NASB)

God does not force us to come to Him. Rather we have been given free will to either accept or reject His amazing offer. Grace is a free gift offered to us by God, through Jesus, by turning to Him in faith. If you do so, your sins will be forgotten, and you will have eternal life. Death is an instantaneous appointment when you step into eternity. It may very well happen at the moment you least expect it.

It is important to understand the reality that there are physical laws which are true and there are spiritual laws which are true. For example, if I am holding a hockey puck in my hand and I let go, what will happen? It will fall right down to the ice because of gravity. We have never seen gravity, but we believe in it. We have not seen gravity, but we have seen the effects of gravity. These are truths of physics. In the same way, there are spiritual truths. We can see the effects of spiritual truths in people whose lives have been dramatically changed when they became Born-Again Christians.

A major spiritual truth is that with death comes eternity. There only two destinations. One destination is heaven, which is available to everyone who puts their faith and trust in Jesus. The only other destination is a horrific place called hell. The Bible is clear about how terrible it is through the frightening words of Jesus:

> In that place there will be weeping and gnashing of teeth...
> Luke 13:28 (ESV)

It is a place of separation from God forever and ever, and ever, and ever.... Another scripture explains the trauma:

They will be punished with everlasting destruction and shut out from the presence of the Lord and from the glory of his might. 2 Thessalonians 1:9 (NIV)

Eternity is a very long time...

Stan Mikita passed away a couple of years ago. When I heard Gordie Howe was close to death, I sent him a card of encouragement. Enclosed in the card was a Bible tract which outlined what is described above and is known as the Gospel of Jesus Christ. I don't know what Howe's spiritual condition was at the time. It is my hope that if he did not know Jesus then, that he read the tract and accepted the free gift of eternal life. If he did, I will meet him one day in heaven.

You have a choice. You can choose to ignore the life, the love, the warning, the death, the resurrection, and the claims of Jesus Christ. If you do, you will die in your sins. God will judge every person for their sins because God is holy and righteous and just.

Or you can choose the Gospel, which means the "Good News." You can turn to Jesus in faith. When you do, you become a Born-Again Christian whose sin debt is paid. The Born-Again Christian does not need to fear death because their sins do not have to be judged; their sins have been removed and forgotten. When God looks upon a Christian, He will see the righteousness of Christ which covers them.

Since Jesus has done all the work needed to satisfy God's wrath over sin by dying on the cross, we have absolutely no bragging rights. The Apostle Paul makes this clear:

> For it is by grace you have
> been saved, through faith; and
> that not of yourselves, it is the gift
> of God; not as a result of works, so
> that no one may boast. Ephesians
> 2:8-9 (NASB)

Finally, a famous verse from the Bible sums it all up:

> For God so loved the world,
> that He gave His only begotten

Son, that whoever believes in Him
shall not perish, but have eternal
life. John 3:16 (NASB)

When we know Jesus, when we turn away from sin and turn to Him in faith, the gates of heaven are swung wide open for us. Jesus does it all for you because God loves you more than you can ever possibly imagine!

Chapter 10
Real Champions

The Blackhawks won the Stanley Cup in 1934, in 1938, and then again in 1961. Then came a very long and parched drought lasting forty-nine years. Hockey phenom Patrick Kane ended that drought with an overtime game-winning goal against the Philadelphia Flyers in 2010. Two more Stanley Cup Championships were to follow soon after in 2013 and in 2015. It has been an unbelievable run of heart-pounding joy for me. Yet, we are on this earth only for a short season. All the events described in this book seem like they just happened yesterday because this mortal life goes by so fast.

I still play hockey. At the end of each season I think maybe this will be my last go around. Yet I keep on signing up for another season. The championship game is still out there. It calls me as if it is unfinished business.

After vowing to learn about the Bible three decades ago, and reading it so diligently, the Holy Spirit really got hold of me and my life. As I read the Scriptures, I knew that it was all true. And since it was all true, my life had to change and reflect those truths. As I learned to pray and ponder what those changes in my life might look like, the Lord raised the bar for me – so much so that one day He called me to be a pastor. My Divine instructions were clear: "Answer the call to become a pastor and lead other people to Me for the rest of your life!" I was 29 at the time. The same number I had on my college jersey and the same number on my belated hockey trophy.

Thus my wife and I walked away from the comfortable life and powerful trappings which corporate America can provide. We did so in order to be able to fully serve the Lord Jesus Christ and to lead people to the truth of His gospel of salvation. We made a commitment to be *all in*. There were many sacrifices along the way, only to be outweighed by the joy of following Christ.

The Christian life is heavy at times, but it is worth it. The Christian life is also exciting. Ministry has allowed me to serve my fellow man in local churches; in jails, prisons, and detention centers; in hospitals and nursing homes. Evangelism and mission work have taken me to nine different countries on seventeen mission trips. Consider one example of how exhilarating ministry life with Jesus can be...

I was street preaching in a public square in the Dominican Republic. My good friend and trusted Spanish translator, Esthervin, was repeating every word that went out. We were standing on a small, concrete bell-shaped platform which was about four feet tall. Ironically, my initials were spray-painted on the side. Throngs of people were gathering around the platform.

As we preached the Word of God, two men appeared out of the large crowd. They came forward right in front of us with their heads bent down so we never saw their faces. Each one had an arm up with an open palm signifying they were praying over us. After we finished preaching, I gave an invitation for anyone to come and receive Jesus as their Lord and Savior. We slowly turned around on the platform, making the invitation to all segments of the crowd. After we completed our 360, we heard these words, "Our friend here wishes to receive Jesus into his heart."

As Esthervin was speaking, I noticed that the two men who were praying directly in front of us were gone. I quickly scanned the crowd. They were nowhere to be seen, although it seemed impossible that they could have worked their way out of so many people. I intently asked Esthervin, "Who were those guys?" It was a mystery. We both felt as if help had been sent to us from above.

We climbed down onto the street to meet the man who was ready to turn his life over to Christ. The man who spoke up continued, "This is Juan, and he wants to have Jesus today." Juan stood there with tears in his eyes. We were then introduced to two other men who were standing there with him. All three of Juan's friends were carrying Bibles. The same man spoke again, "Pastor this is a miracle!"

I agreed, "You know any time someone comes to Jesus to repent of sin and give their life to Him, it is a miracle."

"Oh pastor," he said. "You don't understand. We have been praying for Juan's salvation for ten years, and today he receives Jesus."

We prayed with Juan and then I left instructions for his three friends: "I am only visiting your country so I will not be here to disciple your friend going forward. It has to be all of you."

"Yes sir!" was the reply. "We will be doing it!"

There are so many more glorious stories like this I could write about, but I will let you have your own encounters of the work of the Holy Spirit of God. You can choose to be on the winning team which has defeated death. It is my hope and prayer that you will make that choice to be a real champion.

When you become a Born-Again Christian, you will find meaning and purpose in your life and you will be living for something much greater than yourself. You may not be called to be a pastor or missionary, but you can be sure that God has a glorious plan for your life. There will be bumps in the road, but it will be exciting, and it will be worth it.

Thank you for allowing me to share my spiritual journey as it relates to my favorite sport. I hope my story provides answers to some of your own questions. If you are ready to accept God's free gift of salvation, the next page provides a prayer so that you can receive Jesus Christ as your Savior.

Pray this prayer from the depth of your soul:

Dear Jesus,

I   (your name here)   know that I am a sinner. Right now, I make that confession to You, and I ask You to come into my life. I know I have broken Your laws and that I could never be good enough to enter heaven by anything I could do. I want to have my sins washed away by your precious blood from the cross. Please let your Holy Spirit come into me and let me now live the life that You would have me live. My life is now all yours.

Thank you, Jesus, for saving me!

If you have prayed this prayer, praise God! Your next step is to find a local church which preaches and teaches the true Word of God. Talk to the pastor and tell him of your new relationship with Jesus. Connect with the local church and attend and support it – not because you have to, but because you want to.

I will keep playing hockey as long as I can. I will keep following the Blackhawks as long as I can. Then, when it's all said and done, I will be watching from the skybox in heaven because I became a Born-Again Christian. And just maybe, Grampa Bruni figured it all out and gave his life to Christ before he passed on. If so, we will have some catching up to do.

What about you? Will you take that step of turning to Jesus? I am praying that you will. Then one day I will meet you in heaven, too.

Please feel free to email me if you have any questions about the gospel of Jesus Christ.

terryamann@hotmail.com.

CPSIA information can be obtained
at www.ICGtesting.com
Printed in the USA
LVHW091229171220
674414LV00005B/796